D1561313

Towards the Eternal Center
Israel, Jerusalem and the Temple

An Exhibition

March 5 - June 27, 1996

The Library

of

The Jewish Theological Seminary of America

New York City

This publication is issued in conjunction with the exhibition *Towards the Eternal Center: Israel, Jerusalem and the Temple,* which was held at the Library of The Jewish Theological Seminary of America from March 5, 1996 to June 27, 1996.

Exhibition Curators: Sharon Liberman Mintz and Elka Deitsch
Research Associate: Yisrael Dubitsky
Cover Design: Paul Davis Studio
Photography: Suzanne Kaufman
Production: Rickie Weiner
Printer: Kensington House Publishing Ltd.

ISBN 0-87334-072-8

© The Library of The Jewish Theological Seminary of America, 1996.

Front Cover image
    Outer Circle: Detail of Hebrew Map of Israel from *Haggadah,* Amsterdam, 1712
    Middle Circle: Detail of Elijah Leading the Messiah into Jerusalem from *Maḥzor,* Corfu, 1709
    Inner Circle: Detail of Map of Jerusalem with Images of the Temple, England, 18th century

Title Page image
    Detail of Hebrew Map of Israel from *Haggadah,* Amsterdam, 1712

This publication was made possible by The Friends of the Library
and the Arthur Rubloff Residuary Trust.
Additional funding was provided by Mr. Gershon Kekst
in honor of the birth of Mr. & Mrs. Lester Pollack's grandchildren.

Preface

The Library of the Jewish Theological Seminary was founded with a mission to be the National Museum of the Jewish Book, and is the premier research library in Judaica and Hebraica. Its collection of manuscripts, incunabula, genizah fragments, broadsides, ketubbot, megillot and sixteenth to eighteenth century Hebrew books is an invaluable and necessary tool for any scholar or student of the Jewish heritage. It is the goal of the Library to conserve the Jewish past to build the Jewish future.

The Friends of the Library has provided funding for a program of exhibitions at the Library. The purpose of this program is to enable the public to get to know and see the vast treasures of the Jewish heritage that the Library has collected over the years.

The exhibit, *Towards the Eternal Center: Israel, Jerusalem and the Temple* brings together different types of materials from the Library's collection. Medieval manuscripts, books printed in Jerusalem, maps, postcards depicting scenes of Jerusalem, illuminations from eighteenth century manuscripts, prints of Jerusalem and Mizrah broadsides are woven together to show the history of Jerusalem and its importance to the Jewish people. The record of this exhibit is being published in order to make these various materials available to the public.

As part of the worldwide celebration of Jerusalem 3000, the Library decided to mount this exhibit. However, the recent tragic event of the assassination of Prime Minister Yitzhak Rabin has prompted us to dedicate this catalog to his memory. Yitzhak Rabin will always be remembered and revered for dedicating his life to the State of Israel. But in his capacity as Commander-in-Chief of the Israel Defense Forces he reunited Jerusalem and established Jewish sovereignty over the most important city in Jewish history and tradition. It is therefore very fitting that this catalog is published in his memory. יהי זכרו ברוך

The exhibit benefitted greatly from the work of its curators, Ms. Sharon Liberman Mintz, Assistant Curator of Jewish Art at the Library, and Ms. Elka Deitsch who conceived, researched and implemented this important exhibit. We are indebted to them.

The Arthur Rubloff Residuary Trust and the Friends of the Library made possible the printing of this catalog. Additional funding was also provided by Mr. Gershon Kekst in honor of the birth of grandchildren to Mr. and Mrs. Lester Pollack.

We also wish to thank Dr. David A. and Lillian Salwen Abramson for their loan of maps that enriched the exhibit.

This catalog is part of a series of catalogs that document the treasures of the Jewish heritage at the Library.

Dr. Mayer E. Rabinowitz
Librarian

December 21, 1995

Address by Prime Minister Yitzhak Rabin Inaugurating Jerusalem 3000 Festivities

Jewish legend tells us that at the moment that King David was about to dig the foundations of the Holy Temple, the groundwaters rose and threatened to flood and destroy Jerusalem, the land of Israel and the entire world.

The legend goes that King David then rose and cast into the turbulent waters a shard on which the Ineffable Name of God was written and the waters immediately receded. The People of Israel were assured safety in their land and on their soil.

If it were only possible to repeat that feat today. I would write on that shard two words of love to Jerusalem, to the land of Israel. One word, tolerance. The other, peace.

Sons and daughters of Jerusalem, I am a Jerusalemite.

I was born in Sharei Zedek hospital in Jerusalem. In Jerusalem, I was a partner as a soldier and a commander in the bitter battles of the War of Independence. In Jerusalem, I saw my friends and my soldiers lose their lives facing the walls that fell to the Arab Legion.

In Jerusalem, I had the great privilege to be in command during the Jewish people's finest hour when, during the Six-Day War, the Temple Mount was liberated. In Jerusalem today, we are now carrying out the battle for peace.

Yes, I am a Jerusalemite.

Three thousand years of history look down upon us today, here, in the city whose streets were trampled by Greek phalanxes, whose pavements were trodden on by Roman legions whose catapults tried to breach its walls, whose inhabitants were vanquished by the Crusaders, here where Turkish cavalry galloped through the streets and where British officers peered out from their forts.

Three thousand years of history look down upon us today, in the city from whose stones the ancient Jewish nation sprang, from whose clear mountain air three religions absorbed their spiritual essence and their strength. Jerusalem, to which every believing Jew turns three times a day in the prayer "May our eyes behold Your return to Zion in mercy."

Three thousand years of history look down upon us today, as do the dreams which cover the hyssop of the Western Wall and the silent graves of the Mount of Olives and Mount Herzl; the hush of the footsteps of the pilgrims and the thunder of the nailed boots of the ruthless conquerers; whose walls resonate with the prayers of the children and the pleas of the praying; where the exultation of victory mingled with the tears of the paratroopers next to the remnants of the temple, liberated from the yoke of strangers.

Three thousand years of dream and prayer today wrap Jerusalem in love and bring close Jews of every generation, from the fires of the Inquisition to the ovens of Auschwitz, and from all corners of the earth, from Yemen to Poland.

Three thousand years of Jerusalem are for us, now and forever, a message for tolerance between religions of love between peoples, of understanding between the nations, of the penetrating awareness that there is no State of Israel without Jerusalem, and no peace without Jerusalem united, the City of Peace. On the day that the Government Offices were moved to Jerusalem, on December 13, 1949, the first Prime Minister, David Ben Gurion said, "The State of Israel has, and will have, only one capital, Eternal Jerusalem. So it was 3000 years ago and so it will be, as we believe for eternity."

United Jerusalem is the heart of the Jewish people and the capital of the State of Israel. United Jerusalem is ours. Jerusalem forever!

Jerusalem, September 4, 1995.

Yitzhak Rabin
1922-1995

This publication is dedicated to the memory of Prime Minister Yitzhak Rabin

מוקדש לזכרו של ראש ממשלת ישראל יצחק רבין ז"ל

Introduction

ארץ ישראל יושבת באמצעיתו של עולם, וירושלים באמצע ארץ ישראל, ובית המקדש באמצע ירושלים. . .

The Land of Israel is situated in the center of the world, and Jerusalem in the center of the Land of Israel, and the Holy Temple in the center of Jerusalem . . .
(Midrash Tanḥuma, Kedoshim 10)

This expressive midrash characterizes three spiritual centers of the world upon which countless generations of Jews have projected their hopes and dreams. The desire to reach these centers permeates almost every aspect of Judaism: its thought, custom and liturgy. The importance of these locations is emphasized even in the rules governing prayer; Jews in the Diaspora face Israel, Jews in Israel face Jerusalem and Jews in Jerusalem face the Temple.

In an heroic effort to capture the physical and spiritual significance of these three centers, scholars, travelers and inhabitants of the Holy Land have produced a vast array of manuscripts, printed books, letters, prints and maps. These tangible artifacts of Israel, Jerusalem and the Temple serve as more than geographical descriptions or historical records; their many variations reveal the chroniclers' desire to synthesize the temporal and the spiritual. When the noted French author René Chateaubriand entered Jerusalem in 1806 he poetically described this gap between a physical report and a spiritual perception and he reflected on the difficulty of a complete description of Jerusalem.

> *Then I understood what the historians and travelers reported of the surprise of the Crusaders and pilgrims at their first sight of Jerusalem. I am certain that whoever has had the patience, as I did, to read nearly two hundred modern accounts of the Holy Land, the rabbinic collections, and the passages of the ancients on Judea, would still understand nothing. I stood there, my eyes fixed on Jerusalem, measuring the heights of its walls, recalling all the memories of history from Abraham to Godfrey of Bouillon ... If I were to live a thousand years, never would I forget this wilderness which still seems to breathe with the grandeur of the Lord and the terrors of death.*

Pictorial representations and descriptive works attempt to capture the full spirit of a land that for so long has been the subject of such varying expectations; even a consensus of its history is impossible to come by. This exhibition views the Holy Land through an exploration of the images and words created during the last six centuries. *Towards the Eternal Center* is divided into three sections: Israel depicted in maps, Jerusalem represented in manuscripts, rare printed books and postcards, and the Temple depicted in prints and mizraḥs.

Israel

Despite the development of a scientific approach towards map-making, it should be remembered that maps are a cartographic representation of a reality. Maps may be viewed as a form of visual communication, a rhetoric of symbols used to express spatial, territorial, political and religious relationships. Color, shape and composition communicate as much about the community for which these maps were produced as the space they describe. Maps of the Holy Land often served as guides for religious history, illustrating biblical episodes, the territorial boundaries of the Twelve Tribes and the wanderings of the Jews in the desert. Maps produced for Christians illustrated holy sites and assisted pilgrims and travelers in their journeys.

Jerusalem

Jewish and Christian travel literature reveals invaluable social histories regarding the living conditions, inhabitants and perils of traveling in medieval Europe and the Middle East. Rabbinic texts produced in Jerusalem attest to the continuing role of the Holy City as a spiritual center even during times of abject poverty and persecution. Accounts of daily life: letters, pleas for assistance and yeshiva annals provide significant historical records. Charming and imaginative visions of Jerusalem executed by Jewish scribe/artists of Europe appear in a selection of illuminated eighteenth-century manuscripts. The expanding culture of Jerusalem is manifest in the resurgence of Jerusalem's printing industry in the nineteenth century and in the colorful depictions of the city and its inhabitants in late-nineteenth and early-twentieth century postcards.

The Temple

The image of the Temple is virtually impossible to separate from the concept of Jerusalem. The belief that a rebuilt Temple signifies the Messianic era, a time when the city of Jerusalem will be the center of the world, permeates the philosophy of Judaism. Whether shown in schematic prints or micrographic mizraḥs, as the Temple of Solomon or as the Third Temple to be built in the time of the Messiah, the image of the Temple has remained woven into the fabric of the culture of the Jewish people.

Sharon Liberman Mintz and Elka Deitsch, *Curators*

Israel

Maps

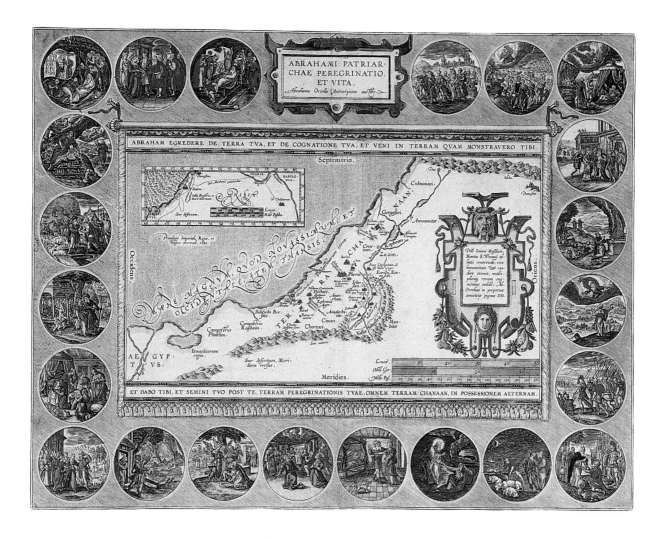

1. **Abrahami Patriarchae Peregrinatio Et Vita**
(The Journey and Life of Abraham the Patriarch)
Abraham Ortelius
Antwerp, ca. 1590
49 x 60.8 cm
[On Loan from Dr. David A. and Lillian Salwen Abramson]

Abraham Ortelius (1527-1598), a cartographer from Antwerp, is credited with assembling the first systematic compilation of maps. In the twenty-two roundels that surround the image of the Land of Canaan, this famous map chronicles the life and travels of the Patriarch Abraham. The map within the map, in the upper left-hand corner, traces Abraham's route from Mesopotamia to Shechem, Israel.

Maps

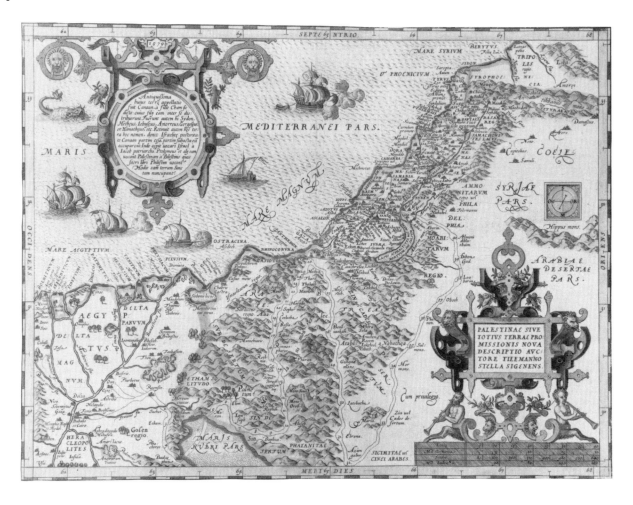

2. **Palestinae Sive Totius Terrae Promissionis Nova Descriptio . . .**
(A New Description of Palestine, that is the Entire Promised Land)
Abraham Ortelius
Printed by Christopher Plantin
Antwerp, 1584
44.8 x 55 cm
[On Loan from Dr. David A. and Lillian Salwen Abramson]

Ortelius' maps became the standard for seventeenth-century map makers. He was the first cartographer to assemble uniformly-sized maps of all the known lands of the world. He published these maps in book format in his magnum opus *Theatrum Orbis Terrarum* (Theater of the Terrestrial Sphere). This map of the Holy Land, Syria, Arabia, and parts of Egypt and the Sinai peninsula was reproduced in *Theatrum Orbis Terrarum* and is based on an earlier map by Tilemannus Stella (1525-1589).

Maps

3. **Ierusalem Moderne**
(Modern Jerusalem)
Alain Manesson Mallet
Printed by D. Thierry
Paris, 1683
21 x 14 cm
[On Loan from
Dr. David A. and Lillian
Salwen Abramson]

Mallet (1630-1706) was a French cartographer and engineer who published his extensive description of the world in the five-volume work *Description de l'univers* . . . . This map is a birds-eye, eastern view of "modern" Jerusalem as it was thought to have appeared in the time of the Ottoman Empire. At bottom, beneath the Kidron river, Mallet depicts a group of Moslems praying.

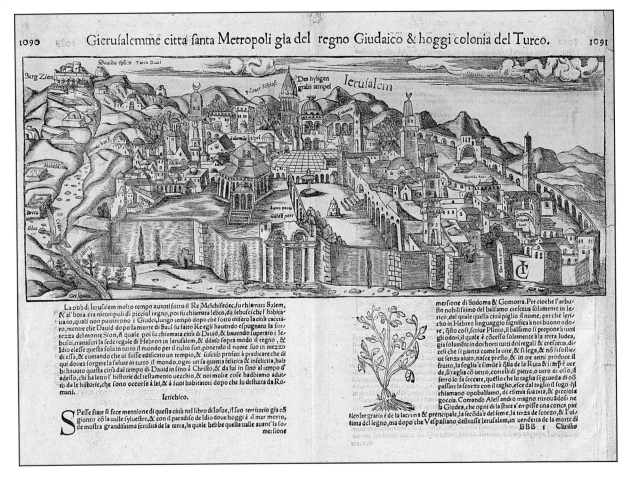

4. Gierusalemme citta santa Metropoli gia del regno Giudaico & hoggi colonia del Turco
(The Holy City of Jerusalem, a Metropolis During the Kingdom of Judah, now a Colony of the Turks)
Sebastian Münster
Drawn by Jacob Clauser
Basel?, 1558?
Printed by Heinrich Petri?
30.9 x 39 cm
[On Loan from Dr. David A. and Lillian Salwen Abramson]

Sebastian Münster (1488-1552) was an important sixteenth-century German Christian Hebraist, a prolific author and a translator of important Hebrew texts. In addition, Münster was a mathematician, cosmographer and cartographer. This imaginary view of Jerusalem was published in his magnum opus, *Cosmographia.* First printed in 1544, this work comprised a comprehensive description of the world and was reprinted thirty-six times in only one hundred years. Münster's book was originally published with over four hundred woodcuts of city views, maps, portraits and costumes.

Maps

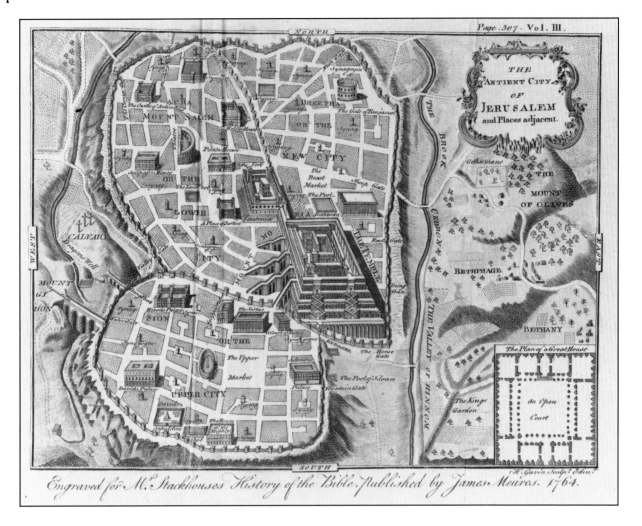

5. **The antient [sic] City of Jerusalem and Places adjacent**
Engraved by H. Gavin
Printed by James Meuvos
London, 1764
20.1 x 32.6 cm
[On Loan from Dr. David A. and Lillian Salwen Abramson]

Thomas Stackhouse (1706-1784) published this map of Jerusalem and its surroundings in his work *History of the Bible*. Stackhouse was a British historian, geographer and publisher of religious texts. An oversized image of the Temple is prominently placed in the center of the map. Stackhouse incorporated major biblical and historical sites of ancient Jerusalem, including the gates of the city and Herod's Palace.

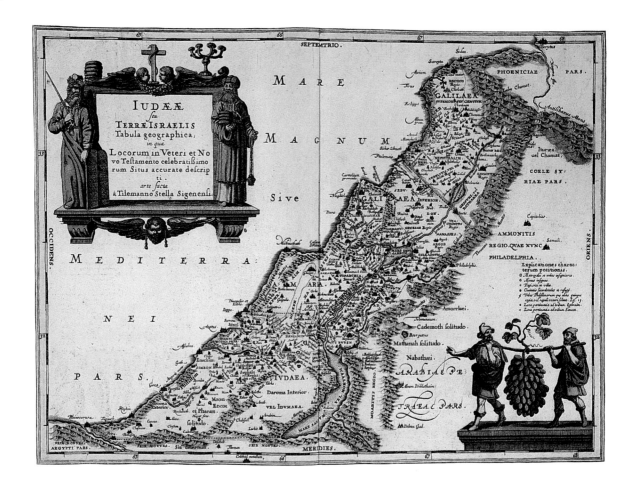

6. Iudaeae seu Terrae Israelis Tabula geographica; in qua Locorum in Veteri et Novo Testamento celebratissimorum Situs accurate descripti

(Geographical Table of Judea, that is the Land of Israel, in which the More Famous Places in the Old and New Testament are Accurately Described)

Georg Horn
London, 1741
59.5 x 50 cm
[On Loan from Dr. David A. and Lillian Salwen Abramson]

Georg Horn (1620-1670), a Dutch historian and geographer, based this map on an earlier engraving by Tilemannus Stella. In the lower right-hand corner, the two spies sent by Moses, Joshua and Caleb, are shown carrying an enormous bunch of grapes as mentioned in Numbers 13:23. Moses, his hand resting on the Tablets of the Law, and his brother Aaron, holding implements of the Temple, frame the title cartouche.

**7. Iudaea sive Terra Sancta quae Israelitarum in suas duodecim tribus
destincta secretis ab invicem regnis Iuda et Israel**
(The Land of Judea, that is the Holy Land of the Israelites -
The Twelve Tribes Shown in the Kingdom of Judah and Israel)
Theodorus Danckerts
Amsterdam, ca. 1680
51.8 x 53.4 cm
[On Loan from Dr. David A. and Lillian Salwen Abramson]

The Danckerts were a Dutch family of engravers and map publishers. They produced
maps in Amsterdam for almost an entire century (1660 to 1720). A legend at the lower
right-hand corner of this map designates symbols for selected cities, including cities of
refuge, and the cities of the Levites. The High Priest beneath the title panel is depicted
preparing an incense offering on the Golden Altar.

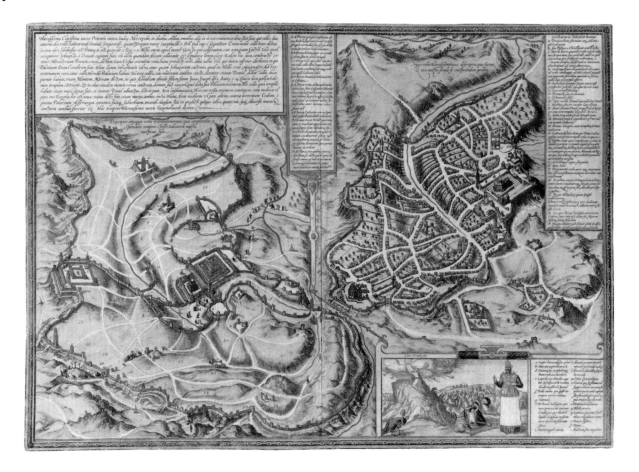

8. **Hierosolyma, Clarissima totius Orientis civitas, Iudaee Metropolis . . . Hoc tempore Hierosolyma turcis Cuzumobarech dicitur**
(Jerusalem, "Pearl of the Orient", Capitol of Judea . . .
Now Known as the Jerusalem of Cuzumobarech the Turk)
Frans Hogenberg
Cologne, 1574
19.8 x 40.3 cm
[On Loan from Dr. David A. and Lillian Salwen Abramson]

This map depicting two plans of Jerusalem was published in Georg Braun and Frans Hogenburg's *Beschreibung und Contrafactur der Vornembsten Stät der Welt.* "Modern" Jerusalem is illustrated on the right and an imaginary geographical description on the left depicts Jerusalem in the time of Jesus. Frans Hogenburg (1535-1590) was a noted Flemish engraver, cartographer and map publisher who is credited with engraving many of Abraham Ortelius' maps.

Maps

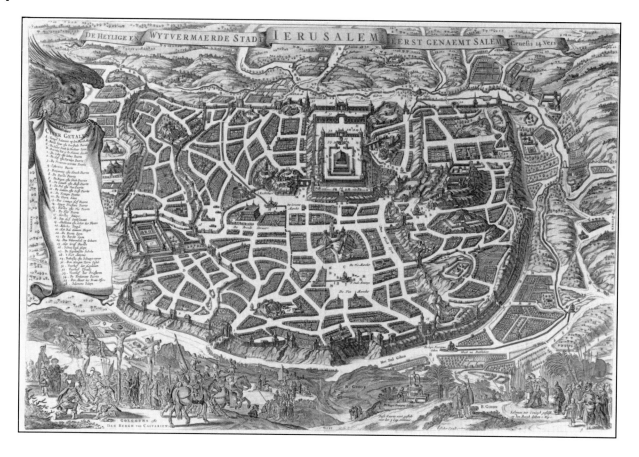

9. **De Heylige en wytvermaerde stadt Ierusalem, eerest Genaemt Salem. Genesis 14. Vers 18**
(The Holy and Very Famous State of Jerusalem which is called Salem in Genesis 14:18)
Nicolas Visscher
Holland, 1690
33 x 49 cm
[On Loan from Dr. David A. and Lillian Salwen Abramson]

This imaginary map of ancient Jerusalem prominently depicts the Second Temple in the center of the city. The title of the map, which identifies Jerusalem as Salem, is based on the biblical verse: "And King Melchizedek of Salem brought out bread and wine; he was priest of God Most High." The lower right-hand corner contains an illustration of the anointment of King Solomon and on the left, the crucifixion of Jesus at Golgotha on Calvary. Four generations of the Visscher family produced maps and prints in Holland, from the sixteenth to the eighteenth century.

Maps

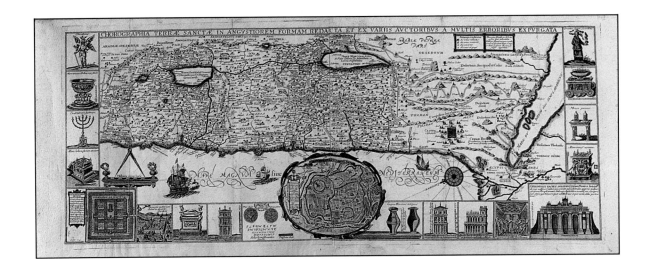

10. Chorographia Terrae Sanctae in angustiorem formam redacta, et ex variis auctoribus a multis erroribus expurgata

(Outlay of the Holy Land Printed in Narrow Format with Numerous Corrections Made by Various Authors)
Jacobus Tirinus
Engraved by Cornelius Galle?
Printed by Martinus Nutius
Antwerp, 1632
37.9 x 92.4 cm
M 35

This hand-colored, printed map appeared within Jacobus Tirinus' book *Commentarius in Vetus et Novum Testamentum* (Commentary on the Old and New Testament). Oriented towards the east, the map includes the territories of the twelve tribes on both sides of the Jordan River. The inset oval map in the lower margin features a reproduction of an earlier view of ancient Jerusalem created by the sixteenth-century Spanish, biblical geographer, Juan Bautista Villalpando (1552-1608).

Maps

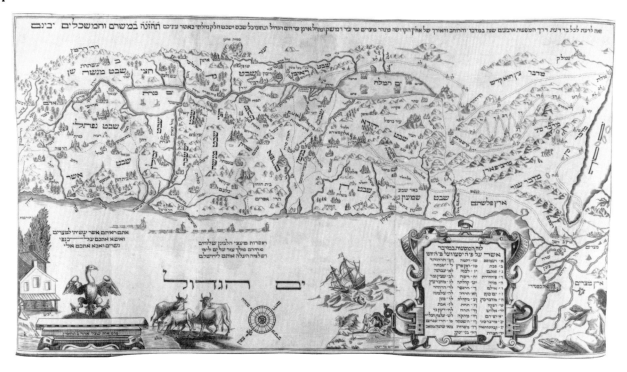

11. . . . Derekh ha-Massa'ot Arba'im Shanah ba-Midbar ve-ha-Roḥav ve-ha-Orekh shel Ereẓ ha-Kedoshah . . .

(Route of the Forty-Years Journeys and the Length and Breadth of the Holy Land)
Drawn by Abraham bar Jacob
Printed by Solomon Proops
Amsterdam, 1712
26 x 47.9 cm
BM 675.P4 A3 1712

This map, one of the earliest Hebrew maps extant, was originally published in the Amsterdam Haggadah of 1695 (see no. 40). The artist, Abraham bar Jacob, was a German preacher who converted to Judaism and resided in Amsterdam. The map contains biblical verses that accompany several illustrations: boats carrying cedarwood from Tyre for the building of the Temple, scenes of Jonah and the Whale and cows and beehives illustrating Israel as the Land of Milk and Honey. The exodus from Egypt is represented by an eagle with spread wings, reflecting the biblical words: "You have seen what I did to the Egyptians, how I bore you on eagles' wings and brought you to me" (Exodus 19:4). In the lower right-hand corner, the forty-one encampments of the Jews in the desert are listed.

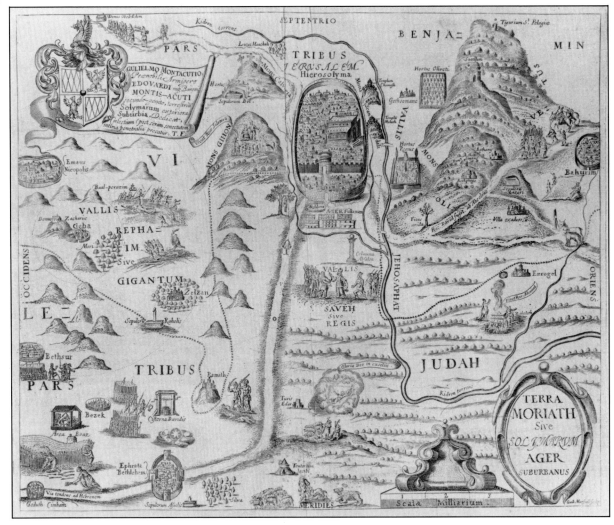

12. Terra Moriath sive Solymarum ager suburbanus
(The Land of Moriah, or the Environs of Jerusalem)
Thomas Fuller
Printed by John Williams
London, 1650
34 x 40.5 cm
M 118

Fuller (1608-1661) was an English scholar and preacher whose historical work on the Bible, *A Pisgah sight of Palestine*, serves as an invaluable cartographic resource. This map entitled *The Land of Moriah* contains a view of the walled city of Jerusalem, an enlarged, romanticized depiction of the Mount of Olives and many biblical landmarks. Each of the maps from Fuller's series contains a coat of arms of the patron who funded publication of the map. The family emblem of Gulielmo Montacutio can be seen in the upper left-hand corner.

Maps

13. Situs Terrae Promissionis, S.S. Bibliorum intelligentiam exacte aperiens . . .
(Site of the Holy Land, an Exact Rendering According to the Holy Bible)
Christian van Adrichom and Jodocus Hondius
Engraved by E.S. van Hamersveldt and Solomon Rogier
Printed by Henricus Hondius and Jan Jansonnius
Amsterdam, 1633
46.6 x 55 cm
M 19

The production of this map involved some of the greatest map makers of Holland. Gerardus Mercator (1512-1594), a Flemish cartographer, initiated the term "atlas" for his collection of maps. In 1604, Jodocus Hondius (1563-1611) an eminent map-publisher, acquired the plates of Mercator's *Atlas* and added his own maps, including this one which is based on the work of the Dutch priest and surveyor, Christian van Adrichom (1533-1585). The result was *Atlas ou representation du monde universel . . .* by Gerard Mercator and Jodocus Hondius. The map reproduced here was published by Hondius' son, Henricus and his son-in-law, Jan Jansonnius.

14. **De Veertig-Jaarige Reys-Togten der Kinderen Israels . . .**
(The Forty Year Journey of the Children of Israel)
Pieter van der Aa
Leiden, ca. 1729
32.5 x 78 cm
M 11

Pieter van der Aa (1659-1733) was a publisher who printed primarily maps and atlases. This map, drawn in unusual perspective, traces the path of the Jews through the Sinai peninsula from Egypt into the Land of Israel. It may have been printed in van der Aa's *Galérie Agréable du Monde*, a sixty-six volume work with over three thousand prints.

15. **Peregrinatie ofte Veertich Iarige Reyse der kinderen Israels . . .**
(Peregrination or the Forty Year Journey of the Children of Israel)
Olfert Dapper and Jacob van Muers
Printed by Jacob van Muers
Amsterdam, 1677?
45.7 x 48.9 cm
M 98

Two dramatic episodes from the period of the Jews' travels in the desert flank the image of Moses receiving the Tablets of the Law. On the right, the Jews are cured from a plague when Moses directs their attention to the copper serpent; on the left, Moses is shown hitting the rock to obtain water for the Children of Israel. The map is adapted from an earlier work by Nicolas Visscher.

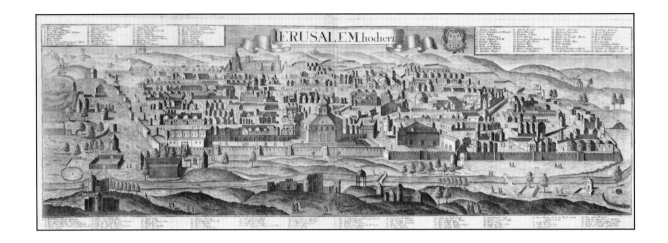

16. **Ierusalem, hodierna**
(Jerusalem, as it is Today)
Georg Balthasar Probst
Drawn by Giovanni Pietro Fabbroni
Printed by the Heirs of Jeremiah Wolff
Augsburg, 1740?
43.2 x 116.7 cm
M 62

This panoramic view of Jerusalem was produced by Probst (1673-1748?), a German copper-engraver and publisher. The Temple of Solomon is modeled after the architecture of The Dome of the Rock. In the upper margins, the Christian holy sites of Jerusalem are listed in Latin, while in the lower margins they are listed in German. The artist has included several figures in order to create a sense of scale.

Jerusalem

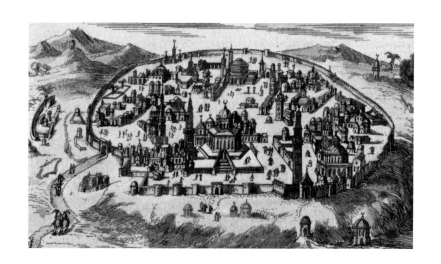

17. Massa'ot shel Rabbi Binyamin/Itinerarium Benjaminis
(The Travels of Rabbi Benjamin)
Benjamin of Tudela
Printed by Bonaventura and Abraham Elzevir
Leiden, 1633
RB 139:12

The travelogue of the Sephardic traveler Benjamin ben Jonah of Tudela is certainly the best known work of all of Jewish travel literature. It serves as the richest source of historical information regarding Jews of the twelfth century. Benjamin began his journey from Saragossa, around the year 1160 and over the course of thirteen years visited a wide range of places including Greece, Syria, Palestine, Mesopotamia and Persia. In his travel diary he described the Jewish population, its customs, education, living conditions and occupations. In addition to his description of Jewish living conditions, Benjamin also reported on the secular politics, commercial welfare and geography of the different countries he visited.

This miniature edition contains both the Hebrew text and a Latin translation by Constantin L'Empereur, a professor of Hebrew at Leiden University during the first part of the seventeenth century.

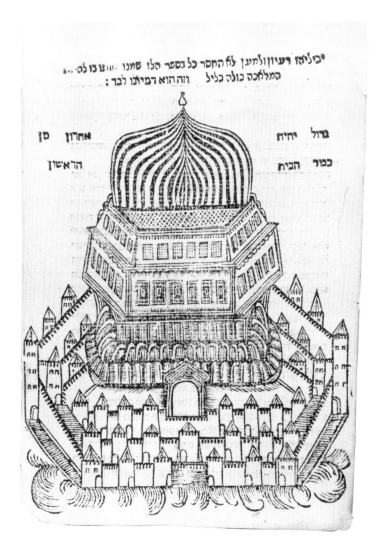

המלאכה כולה כליל וזה הוא דמיונו לבד :

גדול יהיה   כבור הבית

אהרון סן   גדול יהיה

ראשון   כבור הבית

18. Zikhron be-Yerushalayim
(A Remembrance of Jerusalem)
Compiled by Judah Poliastro
Printed by Jonah ben Jacob Ashkenazi
Constantinople, 1743
ms. 5655

This volume contains an eclectic group of texts relating to the Holy Land. In his introduction, Judah
Poliastro notes that he thought it important to com-
pile these writings as they had long been out of print
and unavailable to the Jewish public. Among the
works he includes is a travelogue by Rafael Treves
and selected prayers to be recited at the graves of
the righteous or when standing before the Western
Wall. The book is decorated with four woodcut illustrations including an imaginative vision of the future
Third Temple. The Temple, depicted as an octagonal,
domed structure is flanked by the words *"The glory
of the last will be greater than that of the first."* This
image reflects a tradition which gained popularity
during the Renaissance, when representations of the
Temple were often modeled on the polygonal
structure of the Dome of the Rock, shifting away
from the classical forms used in previous periods.

19. **Shivḥei Yerushalayim**

(In Praise of Jerusalem)
Compiled by Jacob ben Moses Ḥayyim Baruch
Printed by Abraham Isaac Castello and Eliezer Saadon
Livorno, 1785
DS 103.B3 1785 c.2

Shivḥei Yerushalayim, an anthology of travelers' accounts of the Holy Land, was an extremely popular work. The first edition, published in 1785, was followed by no less than eight reprints. Most of this book consists of the travelogue of Moses ben Mordechai Basola, an Italian rabbi and traveler who visited Israel in 1521 and kept a diary of his journey. His writings are one of the earliest descriptions of Israel under the Turkish rule. Pictured here are a group of *takkanot* (regulations) that Basola copied from a chart hanging on the wall of a synagogue in Jerusalem. One of these regulations stipulates that a Jew may not purchase a defective coin; should he receive one accidentally, he may not pass it on to anyone else.

20. Gedenckwaerdige Zee en Landt Voyagie door Europa Asia en America
(A Memorable Sea and Land Voyage
through Europe, Asia and America)
John Sanderson, Henry Timberly
and John Smith
Printed by Jochem van Dyck
Amsterdam, 1678
RB 408:14

Christian pilgrimage to Jerusalem formally began after the Emperor Constantine converted to Christianity in 313 and the Roman Empire adopted Christianity as its religion. In the year 327, Constantine's mother, the Empress Helena, journeyed to the Holy Land and subsequently announced that she had located the true cross and the site of the Holy Tomb. Her discovery fostered a steady stream of pilgrims who came to walk the Via Dolorosa and visit the Church of the Holy Sepulcher, which Constantine had established.

After the Middle Ages, knowledge was increasingly transmitted in written form, resulting in a proliferation of travelogues and itineraries available to the reading public in books. These accounts were penned by pilgrims who went to visit the holy places or by travelers who wandered through Europe, the Orient and the Middle East. They usually consisted of a list of the holy sites, written for both those who would follow in their footsteps and those who would not have the opportunity to ever see the holy sites and would therefore benefit from the vivid descriptions.

In 1601, John Sanderson journeyed to Israel with a group of Jewish pilgrims. His account, was first published in English as part of *Pilgrimes* in London, 1625.

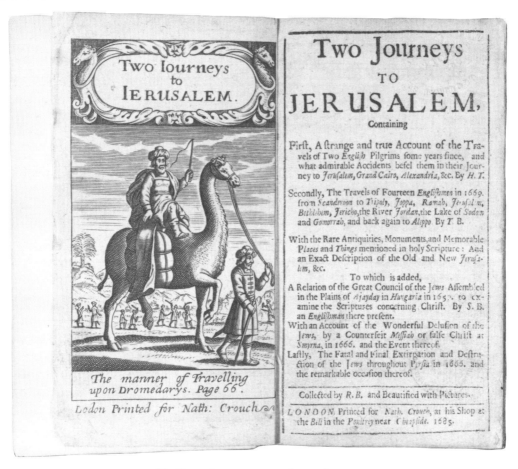

21. **Two Journeys to Jerusalem**
Compiled by Nathaniel Crouch
London, 1685
Printed for Nathaniel Crouch
RB 434:14a

Travel literature remains a rich source of history, topography, civilization, economy, social conditions, and population counts. From the sixteenth through the nineteenth century, approximately 120 travel books were produced by Christian travelers. The primary incentives for pilgrimages were to atone for crimes, gain remission of sins, obtain penance, fulfill vows, cure illnesses, and acquire relics. By the Middle Ages, the religious motives were increasingly replaced by commercial ones. Even in the ninth and tenth centuries the Muslim rulers had encouraged trade in Jerusalem, which had become a commercial meeting point between East and West. Pilgrims were succeeded by travelers looking for adventure, profit and the desire to see foreign lands, people and customs. *Two Journeys to Jerusalem* is a collection of travelogues containing various essays, including the popular *A Strange and True Account of the Travels of Two English Pilgrims* by Henry Timberlake, and a narrative about the seventeenth-century false messiah, Shabbetai Ẓvi. Nathaniel Crouch published this volume under the pseudonym of R.B. (Robert Burton).

22. **Hierusalemsche Reyse**
(Jerusalem Voyage)
Antonius Gonzalez
Printed by Michiel Cnobbaert
Antwerp, 1673
RB 408:4

Gonzalez was a Belgian Franciscan who served in Palestine from 1665 to 1668 as custodian of Bethlehem. Custodians were appointed by the Latin Church to discover and preserve Christian holy sites throughout the Land of Israel. Additionally, they were entrusted with the task of making these sites accessible to pilgrims. Gonzalez's travelogue is divided into six volumes, each describing in great detail a different portion of his voyage. They contain accounts of his journey from Antwerp to Jerusalem, descriptions of the holy places in Israel, visual representations of Syria and Egypt, and an examination of the flora and fauna. The pages reproduced here include a map of "New Jerusalem". Numerical markers indicate various Christian holy sites and other geographical landmarks of Jerusalem. The disproportionally large image of the Temple in the foreground is labeled "Temple of Solomon" but is clearly modeled on the Church of the Holy Sepulcher.

23. Genizah Fragment; Letter from the Crusader Period
20 December 1236
ENA 2559, folio 5

In 1229, forty-two years after the Islamic reconquest of Jerusalem, Frederick II, King of Germany negotiated a treaty with al-Malik al-Kamil, the Sultan of Egypt, which returned everything but the Temple area proper to the control of the Crusaders. During this second period of Crusader rule, which lasted for forty-five years, the Jews were not permitted to live in Jerusalem and were allowed to visit the city only during the festivals.

This thirteenth-century fragment, discovered in the Cairo Genizah, allows us a glimpse into a period of Jewish history of which very little is known. The letter, authored by a traveler to Jerusalem, was sent to his relative in Cairo or Bilbeis (lower Egypt), who was intending to travel to Jerusalem. The anonymous author writes of the one Jew, a painter, who was permitted by the Christian authorities to reside in Jerusalem and the agreement to allow Jews to visit the city of festivals.

24. **Tur Ḥoshen Mishpat**
(Breastplate of Judgement)
Jacob ben Asher
Scribes: Abraham ha-Levi and
Joseph ben Eliezer ha-Sefaradi
Jerusalem, 21 Shevat 5148
(31 January 1388)
R 1118

Jacob ben Asher (also known as the "Ba'al ha-Turim") was a renowned authority on Jewish Law who lived in the late-thirteenth century. He was born in Germany and moved to Toledo at the age of thirty. It was in Spain that he wrote his most famous work, the *Arba'ah Turim,* a compendium of Jewish law and custom. *Tur Ḥoshen Mishpat,* the fourth and final part of the *Arba'ah Turim,* consists of 427 chapters of halakhic rulings relating to civil and criminal law.

According to later sources, Jacob ben Asher set out for Israel in 1340, but died before he could reach his destination. Remarkably, this manuscript was copied in Jerusalem less than fifty years after his death. The surname of the second scribe, Joseph ha-Sefaradi, may indicate that he was among those Jews who fled to Israel in an attempt to escape the escalating persecutions of the Iberian Peninsula. The page reproduced here is part of a section dealing with the laws of selling a field. The illustrations were inserted to help illuminate a difficult portion of the text.

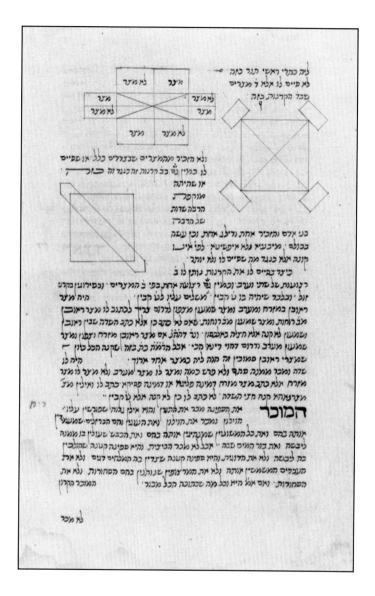

25. Letter from the Rabbis of Jerusalem to the Fez Community Complaining about Extortion and Persecution by Ibn Farukh

Jerusalem, ca. 1629
ms. 3161

This letter was written in the time of the Ottoman rule by the Rabbis of Jerusalem who were desperately requesting funds from the Jews of Fez. It chronicles a bitter period in the history of the Jewish community of Jerusalem that began in 1625 when Muhammad ibn Farukh bought the governorship of Jerusalem. He arrived with three hundred mercenaries and proceeded to terrorize the entire population of the city - Muslim, Christian and Jew. He posted guards at the gates and prohibited everyone from leaving the city. Together with his brother-in-law, Ibrahim Agha, ibn Farukh extorted vast sums of money from the people, forced the Jews to dig ditches around the city walls, kidnapped community leaders for ransom and threatened to vandalize their synagogues. Those who were not able to flee the city went into hiding. Ultimately, ibn Farukh even defied the Sultan Uthman, who sent troops to overthrow the despot. Ibn Farukh, learning of his imminent deposition, took whatever loot he could, kidnapped two Jews, brought them to the synagogue and tortured them before the congregation in order to extort a ransom; he then fled from Jerusalem. The city regained some peace after the reign of ibn Farukh; he had, however, forced the Jewish community into a state of utter destitution from which they would not easily recover.

26. **Derekh Eẓ ha-Ḥayyim**
(The Path of the Tree of Life)
Hayyim ben Joseph Vital
Scribe: Elkanah ben Shimshon ha-Levi
Jerusalem?, 1720
ms. 2178

Ḥayyim Vital (1542-1620), an eminent kabbalist, was born in Israel and began the study of kabbalah at the age of 22. From 1570-1572 he was the principle disciple of Isaac Luria, the leading kabbalist at the time. After Luria's death, Vital attempted to transcribe Luria's teachings, a project that lasted for twenty years as Vital continued to revise and edit his work. He collected his writings into two principal works: *Eẓ ha-Ḥayyim* and *Eẓ ha-Da'at*. Vital carefully controlled access to his books, permitting only a select few to study them. The kabbalists of Palestine regarded Vital's first version of his work *(Mahadurah Kamma)* to be the most authoritative version of the Lurianic system of kabbalah. Vital's son Samuel, who inherited his father's manuscripts, did not allow them to be copied for many years. The title page shown here specifies that the book was copied directly from Vital's manuscript. It is possible, however, that the text of this title page is actually a later copy of an earlier manuscript.

27. Ḥibbat Yerushalayim
(Love of Jerusalem)
Ḥayyim ha-Levi Horowitz
Printed by Israel Bak
Jerusalem, 1844
DS 107.H69 1844 c.1

The first books printed in Israel were produced in Safed between 1577 and 1587. Only six books were printed before this press ceased to operate. Israel Bak (1797-1874), a pioneer, re-established Hebrew printing in Israel and later founded the first Hebrew press in Jerusalem. Bak, who was born in Berdichev, Russia, originally established a publishing house there in 1815. He emigrated to Israel in 1831, bringing with him two presses. Bak began to publish in Safed but eventually moved to Jerusalem after both his business and farm were destroyed by an earthquake in 1837 and again by riots in 1838. The Bak Press remained the only Hebrew press in Jerusalem for twenty-two years and dominated the trade throughout the nineteenth century. The book displayed here contains the well-known printer's mark of the Bak Press depicting the major landmarks of Jerusalem: the Western Wall, the Mount of Olives and the Temple Mount.

Ḥibbat Yerushalayim contains Horowitz's descriptions of the cities of Israel and the holy sites, and provides information about the graves of the righteous. In his introduction, Horowitz lists several earlier travelogues that he had seen and found to contain useful information, including those of Benjamin of Tudela (no. 17) and *Shivḥei Yerushalayim* (no. 19).

28. Sha'alu Shelom Yerushalayim
(Seek the Peace of Jerusalem)
Moses Nehemiah Kahanov
Printed by Abraham Rothenberg and Joel Moses Salomon
Jerusalem, 1868
DS 109.K3 1868

The author of this book, Rabbi Moses Nehemiah Kahanov, emigrated to Jerusalem in 1864 and was asked to head the illustrious Ez Hayyim Yeshiva. In the introduction to this book the author explains that in 1867 it was necessary for him to leave Israel briefly. He grew homesick on the boat and wrote this work to remind himself of the Holy Land. The book was also intended to serve as a source of information about Israel for Jews living outside the land. The text, written in a question and answer format, describes the ethnic origins of the Jewish population of Jerusalem, their occupations, the different yeshivot and the unique prayers, customs and dress of the residents. Although this work was printed anonymously, our copy contains an autographed dedication page from the author to Akiva Lehren, an important financier and member of the Amsterdam Jewish community. It is possible that Lehren, who headed the "Pekidim and Amarkalim Fund", an agency responsible for collecting money for Jews in the Holy Land, provided funds for the publication of this book.

29. Mishpetei ve-Ḥukei Yeshivat Magen Avraham
(Rules and Regulations of Yeshivat Magen Avraham)
Ḥai Raphael Yedidyah Abulafia
Jerusalem, ca. 1850
ms. 3862

The introduction to this volume includes an engaging account of the founding of Yeshivat Magen Avraham. Abulafia, the *Rosh Yeshiva* (director) of this institution recounts that in 1840 when he was traveling on behalf of yeshivot in Jerusalem he met Abraham Senior and convinced him to immigrate to Jerusalem and establish a yeshiva there. Senior had arrived by 1846 and within two years had donated the funds necessary to open the institution. The regulations governing the yeshiva as well as several pages listing the individuals who received stipends for studying at Magen Avraham, are contained within this book.

30. **Letter from Rabbi Samuel Salant, Rabbi Jacob Elyashar, and Rabbi Raphael Meir Panigel to Rabbi Nathan Adler**
15 Elul 5648 (22 August 1888)
ms. 9342

Towards the middle of the nineteenth century, the scarcity of housing in the old city compelled the Jews to seek new areas in which to live. Mishkenot Sha'ananim (tranquil dwellings), the first Jewish quarter to be built outside the city walls was completed in 1860 through the efforts of Sir Moses Montefiore. According to this letter, by 1888 many poor people had erected makeshift huts on a part of the land that had been left empty in this new neighborhood. Considered eyesores by the Turkish authorities, the shacks were summarily torn down, much to the consternation of the inhabitants. Consequently, three eminent rabbinic leaders of Jerusalem wrote to Rabbi Nathan Adler, the Chief Rabbi of Britain and an appointee of the Montefiore family, and requested his help in dealing with the problem.

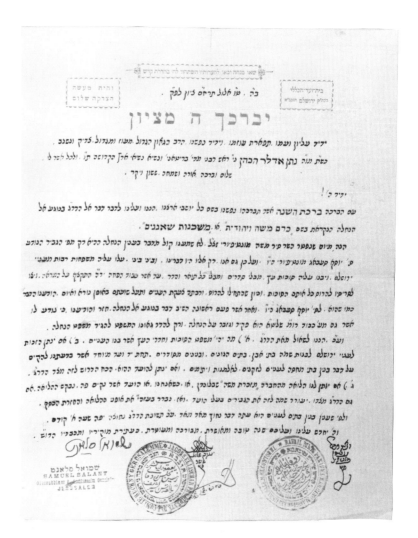

**31. Letter from
Eliezer Lipman Kaminitz
to Elkan Nathan Adler**
London, 20 July 1900
ms. 9342

At the turn of the century, the author of this letter, Eliezer Lipman Kaminitz, owned the finest hotel in Jerusalem. The hotel was founded in 1872 by his father, Menaḥem Mendel. The senior Kaminitz was the author of *Korot ha-Ittim* (Chronicles of the Times); his book includes a detailed first-hand account of the devastation wreaked by the riots of 1834 and the earthquake of 1837. In its early years the hotel had changed locations several times until it finally settled into a new building on Jaffa Road. The letterhead, which bears an image of the edifice, boasts that the building was "constructed on sanitary principle" and provides "the purest water of the whole city". The Kaminitz Hotel was destroyed in the course of the First World War.

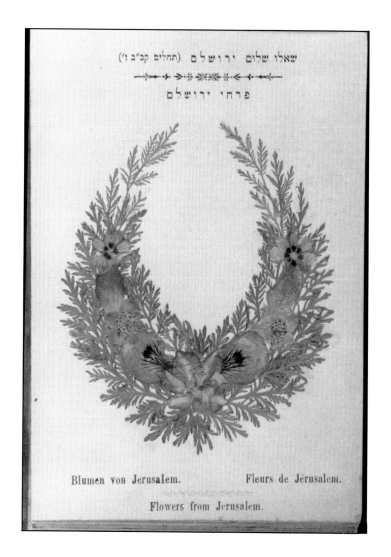

שאלו שלום ירושלם (תהלים קכ"ב ו')

פרחי ירושלם

Blumen von Jerusalem.   Fleurs de Jérusalem.

Flowers from Jerusalem.

32. Pirḥei Ereẓ ha-Kedoshah/ Blumen von Heiligen Lande
(Flowers of the Holy Land)
Jerusalem, ca. 1900

Olive wood-bound volumes containing postcards or dried flowers from Israel have been produced since the late-nineteenth century for travelers of all faiths to take home with them as mementos of their journey to the Holy Land. In this volume, each page is embellished with dried flowers from a different region or holy site in Israel. On the page displayed here, the phrase from Psalms 122:6, *Pray for peace of Jerusalem; May they prosper that love thee,* is placed above an arrangement of flowers from Jerusalem.

ז'ה"ל'צ'"יב
סדר
עבודת הקודש
פעולת צדיק לחיים הרב
הגאון המפו' חיד"א זל"הה
ע"י הרב המדפיס מו"הרר
ישראל ב"ק הי"ו
נדפס פה
עה"ק ירושלים תוב"ב
שנת תר"א לפ"ק

33. Avodat ha-Kodesh
(The Holy Service)
Ḥayyim Joseph David Azulai
Printed by Israel Bak
Jerusalem, 1841
RB 1317:13

Avodat ha-Kodesh, a liturgical work elaborating
on the laws and customs relating to prayer, was
published by Israel Bak. It was the first Hebrew
book to be printed in Jerusalem. Its author,
Ḥayyim Joseph David Azulai (also known by his
acronym as the Ḥida) was a fascinating individual. A noted halakhist, kabbalist and author,
Azulai was born in Jerusalem in 1724. He is
known to have written one hundred and twenty-
six works, of which eighty-two still remain un-
published. In addition, Azulai spent much of
his life traveling to Jewish communities around
the world to raise money for various yeshivot
in Israel.

34. Tefillot Kara'im le-Ḥol ve-Shabbat
(Karaite Prayers for Weekday and Sabbath)
Scribe: Moses ha-Levi ben Abraham ha-Levi
Jerusalem, 27 Kislev 5607 (16 December 1846)
ms. 3406

This prayer book documents the liturgy of the Karaite Jews, also known as the *Ba'alei ha-Mikra* (People of the Scriptures), a sect that arose in the early eighth century. The Karaites base their religious practices entirely upon the written word of the Bible, rejecting the Talmudic and Rabbinic tradition. Originally the Karaites were called Ananites, after their founder Anan ben David who consolidated many varying groups that had arisen during the post-Babylonian era. He implemented extremely stringent observance of traditional Jewish laws such as fasts, circumcision, Sabbath prohibitions and rules of marriage. After Anan's death, the sect fragmented into many splinter groups until the ninth century, when Benjamin ben Moses Nahāwendī unified the Ananites under the name Karaites. Today, Karaite communities are primarily centered in Israel with smaller communities in the United States, Cairo, Istanbul, Poland and Russia.

The Karaite liturgy, which differs from traditional Jewish liturgy, originally consisted of verses from the Bible and encompassed many chapters from Psalms. Eventually it was expanded to include prayers based on the Rabbinic liturgy. Daily prayers are recited only twice a day, in the mornings and evenings.

35. Seder Tefillot bi-Yerushalayim
(The Order of Prayers for Jerusalem)
Jerusalem, 19th century
ms. 8917

This small pamphlet contains the prayers to be recited by a member of the Karaite community who undertakes a pilgrimage to Jerusalem. In the introductory notes the scribe informs us of his desire to assist the pilgrims by gathering these prayers, which were scattered among several sources, into one booklet for ease of use. According to Karaite tradition, pilgrimages were occasions for rejoicing. When the individual began his journey, the entire community would escort him with prayer and song. Also included are specific prayers to be said when approaching the city of Jerusalem and at the graves of various prophets.

36. **Tikhlal**
(Prayer book, Rite of Yemen)
Scribe: Judah Ḥoter ben Aaron ha-Kohen
Jerusalem, 23 Iyar 5651 (31 May 1891)
ms. 4805

This siddur is written according to the rite of the Jews of Yemen. Today, this rite is used only in Israel. The title page states that this volume was written for Naftali (Hermann) Adler, who was chosen in 1891 to succeed his father as Chief Rabbi of Britain (see no. 30). The scribe also notes that in keeping with the tradition found in many ancient Yemenite manuscripts, he has place the vocalization above the text rather than below. In the colophon, the scribe begs forgiveness for any mistakes found in the text and explains that severe time constraints and lack of proper housing made work on this siddur difficult.

37. **Seder Brit Milah**
(Order of Prayers for Circumcision)
Scribe: Jacob ben Isaac
Jerusalem, 1845
ms. 4315

This circumcision book was written for Shimon bar Ya'akov Abrahams in honor of his son's brit. The manuscript contains two introductory poems, the first in honor of Jerusalem and the second in honor of Shimon Abrahams. The latter poem contains Abrahams' first and last name written as an acrostic. The scribe has also indicated the additional text to be recited when the father performs the circumcision.

38. Sefer Shemot
(Book of Exodus)
Jerusalem, 1864
ms. 3463

The Samaritans claim to be descended from the tribes of Ephraim and Menasseh and consider themselves to be the only true followers of the Laws of Moses. Others have suggested that the sect originated in 722 B.C.E. when the Assyrians conquered Samaria and brought in foreigners to colonize the land. Samaritans rely exclusively on the Pentateuch, rejecting the additional books of the Bible (Prophets and Hagiographa). According to their traditions, Mount Gerizim rather than Jerusalem, is the authentic religious center. Today, the Samaritans number less than six hundred and live mainly in Shechem and Ḥolon. They still practice the biblical tradition of sacrifices through the offices of Priests on Mount Gerizim.

Samaritans still employ a modified form of the ancient Hebrew script, known as *Ketav 'Ivri*, as can be seen in this lithographed *Sefer Shemot*. In contrast, after the Babylonian exile, the mainstream Jewish community abandoned this earlier Hebrew script and adopted an Aramaic script known as *Ketav Ashuri*. The Rabbinic authorities wished to distance themselves from this earlier script and ruled that a Torah scroll penned in the "old" Hebrew script does not possess the sanctity of a Torah written in the newer script.

39. **Haggadah**
Mantua, 1560
Printed by Isaac ben Solomon Bassan
at the Press of Giacomo Rufinelli
BM 675.P4 A3 1560

Towards the second half of the fifteenth century, the iconographic motif depicting the arrival of the Messiah appeared in several hand-written illuminated haggadot produced for the Ashkenzic communities of Germany and Northern Italy. This motif illustrated the phrase "Pour out Your fury on the nations that do not know You" (Psalms 79:6), which is recited at the seder when the door is opened and the wine is poured for the cup of Elijah. Drawing upon the pictorial tradition found in manuscripts, this printed volume depicts the prophet Elijah, the traditional herald of the Messiah, blowing a shofar as he leads the Messiah towards Jerusalem's Gate of Mercy.

It was common practice for the producers of printed haggadot to cull typographic and decorative elements from previous editions and to manipulate or elaborate upon them. In this edition, for example, the printer has taken the text from the earlier Prague Haggadah of 1526 and added Italianate floral woodcut borders. The juxtaposition of borrowed and original elements can be seen in both printed and manuscript haggadot over the course of three centuries.

40. **Haggadah**
Amsterdam, 1712
Illustrations by Abraham ben Jacob
Printed by Solomon Proops
BM 675.P4 A3 1712

The Amsterdam Haggadah, first printed in 1695, was the archetype for countless future editions. The splendid quality and remarkably intricate detail of these illustrations was the result of the pioneering use of copper-plate engravings. The artist, Abraham ben Jacob, a convert to Judaism, based his drawings on the biblical images created by Matthaeus Merian for *Icones Biblicae* (published 1625). Inscribed beneath the image of the future Third Temple are the words "The form of the Temple and the city of Jerusalem, may it be speedily rebuilt and re-established in our day". Appended to the end of this volume is the 1712 reprint of one of the earliest Hebrew maps of Israel (see no. 11).

בְּקָרוֹב · בִּמְהֵרָה בִּמְהֵרָה בְּיָמֵינוּ בְּקָרוֹב · אֵל בְּנֵה · אֵל בְּנֵה · בְּנֵה בֵיתְךָ בְּקָרוֹב :
נָדוֹל הוּא · דָּגוּל הוּא · יִבְנֶה בֵיתוֹ בְּקָרוֹב · בִּמְהֵרָה בִּמְהֵרָה בְּיָמֵינוּ בְּקָרוֹב · אֵל
בְּנֵה · אֵל בְּנֵה · בְּנֵה בֵיתְךָ בְּקָרוֹב : הָדוּר הוּא · וָתִיק הוּא · זַכַּאי הוּא · חָסִיד
הוּא · יִבְנֶה בֵיתוֹ בְּקָרוֹב · בִּמְהֵרָה בִּמְהֵרָה בְּיָמֵינוּ בְּקָרוֹב · אֵל בְּנֵה · אֵל בְּנֵה · בְּנֵה בֵיתְךָ
בְּקָרוֹב : טָהוֹר הוּא · יָחִיד הוּא · כַּבִּיר הוּא · לָמוּד הוּא · מֶלֶךְ הוּא · נָאוֹר הוּא ·
סַגִּיב הוּא · עִזּוּז הוּא · פּוֹדֶה הוּא · צַדִּיק הוּא · יִבְנֶה בֵיתוֹ בְּקָרוֹב · בִּמְהֵרָה
בִּמְהֵרָה בְּיָמֵינוּ בְּקָרוֹב · אֵל בְּנֵה · בְּנֵה בֵיתְךָ בְּקָרוֹב : קָדוֹשׁ הוּא · רַחוּם הוּא ·
שַׁדַּי הוּא · תַּקִּיף הוּא · יִבְנֶה בֵיתוֹ בְּקָרוֹב · בִּמְהֵרָה בִּמְהֵרָה בְּיָמֵינוּ בְּקָרוֹב ·
אֵל בְּנֵה · אֵל בְּנֵה · בְּנֵה בֵיתְךָ בְּקָרוֹב :

41. **Haggadah**
Scribe: Joseph ben David Leipnik
Darmstadt, 1733
ms. 4452a

During the eighteenth century there was a remark-
able renaissance in Germany and Central Europe
in the production of Hebrew illuminated manuscripts. Although haggadot were widely available
in numerous, lavishly illustrated, printed editions
(see nos. 39 and 40) manuscript versions were
produced as luxury items, sometimes for wedding
or anniversary gifts. One of the most notable
figures in the eighteenth-century revival of manuscript illumination was a scribe-artist of Moravian
origin, Joseph ben David Leipnik. He produced
at least thirteen skillfully executed illuminated
haggadot between 1731 and 1740. The illustrations of this manuscript are based on the
engravings found in the Amsterdam haggadot
printed in 1695 and 1712 (see no. 40).

42. Seder Birkhat ha-Mazon . . .
im Tikkunei Keriat Shema
Mannheim, 1736
ms. 8230

The charming depiction of Jerusalem illustrates the third benediction of the Grace After Meals, which beseeches God for the rebuilding of the city. Tradition relates that King David and his son Solomon, together, formulated the wording for this blessing. Depictions of Jerusalem during the seventeenth and eighteenth centuries reflect the romantic attitudes about the Holy City. During this period, Jerusalem is rendered with spires and castles grouped together, resembling a prosperous European city rather than a Mediterranean capital. This manuscript, written for Bella of Frankfurt, is testimony to the popular eighteenth-century custom of creating miniature manuscripts for private use.

43. **Haggadah**
Scribe: Issachar Baer ben Jacob Hayyim
Germany?, 1739
ms. 8896

This miniature haggadah contains an unusual illustration of the words, *u-ve-Zero'a Netuyah* (and with an outstretched arm), a phrase from Deuteronomy (26:8) that describes God's might and power when he took the Jews out of Egypt. The haggadah explicates this phrase with a reference to the plague God brought upon Jerusalem in the time of King David. The artist of this volume, however, chose to interpret the phrase in a more positive manner and depicted Sennacherib's thwarted attempt to conquer Jerusalem in 701 B.C.E. instead. The illustration shows an angel with its sword outstretched over Jerusalem protecting the city against the Assyrian forces of Sennacherib. On the folio preceding the illustration, the artist included Talmudic extracts in order to interpret the image: "Is this the city of Jerusalem" he [Sennacherib] exclaimed, "for which I set all my troops in motion and conquered the whole country? Why, is it smaller and weaker than all the cities of all the nations which I have subdued by my might!" *[Babylonian Talmud, Sanhedrin 95a]*. That night all his soldiers were killed. As is stated in Kings II (19:35), "an angel of the Lord went out and smote 185,000 in the Assyrian camp."

44. **Maḥzor Corfu**
Corfu, 1709
ms. 8236

This image of Elijah leading the Messiah into Jerusalem is one of sixteen illustrations that decorate an unusual maḥzor from Corfu. An island off the coast of Greece, Corfu was, for centuries, home to a dynamic Jewish community. The earliest Jewish settlers arrived during the thirteenth century while the island was still under Byzantine rule. These Jews, known as Romaniot, readily adapted many elements of the dominant Greek culture and language.

The manuscript, written in 1709 and completed on the Eve of Shavuot, once belonged to a member of the ancient Romaniot community of Corfu. The Romaniot maintained a separate congregation and attempted to preserve their liturgical rites and customs. In order to ensure that the liturgy would be transmitted correctly, they commissioned scribes to write prayer books that would reflect their traditions.

Postcards of Jerusalem

45. **The Western Wall**

Postcards of Jerusalem

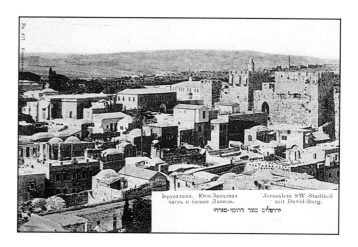

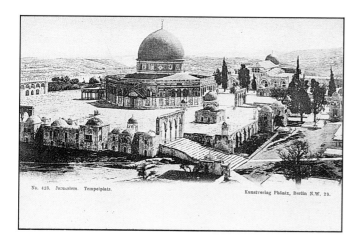

46. **Views of Jerusalem**

47. **Gates of the Old City**

Jerusalem - Bazaar of the Goldsmiths

Die Davidstrasse in Jerusalem　　רחוב דוד בירושלים.

חברת „לבנון" № 215

Strasse in Jerusalem　　רחוב בירושלים.

חברת „לבנון" № 216

JERUSALEM, JAFFA STREET.　　ירושלים רחוב יפו

48. **Streets of Jerusalem**

49. **The People of Jerusalem**

50. **The Bezalel School**

The Temple

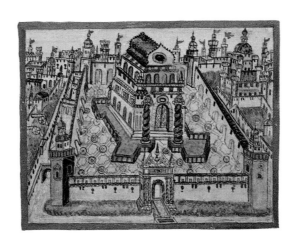

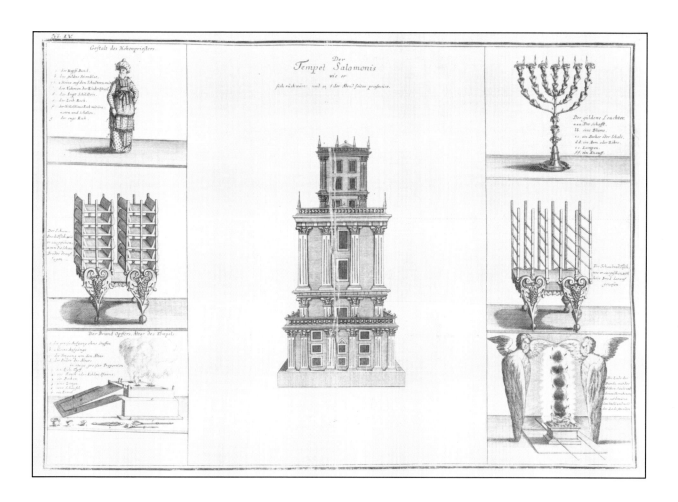

51. **Der Tempel Salomonis**
(The Temple of Solomon)
From *Der Tempel Salomonis*
Printed by Wäysen-Haus
Halle, 1718
RB 416:7a

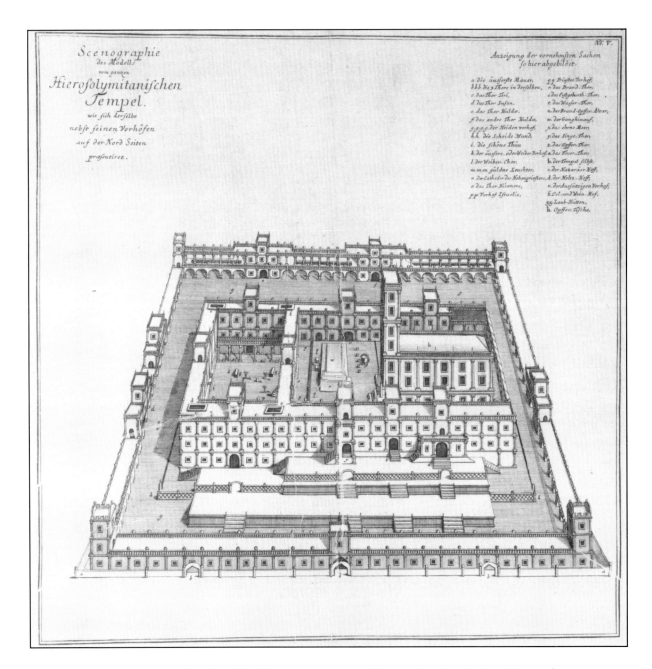

52. Scenographie des Modells von gantzen Hierosolymitanischen Tempel
(A Scene of the Model of the Entire Jerusalem Temple)
From *Der Tempel Salomonis*
Printed by Wäysen-Haus
Halle, 1718
RB 416:7a

53. **Scenographie des eigentlichen Tempels
selbst wie solcher sich auf der Nord-Seiten praesentiret**
(Scenes of the Original Temple as it Appeared from the North Side)
From *Der Tempel Salomonis*
Drawn by I.F.D.
Printed by Wäysen-Haus
Halle, 1718
RB 416:7a

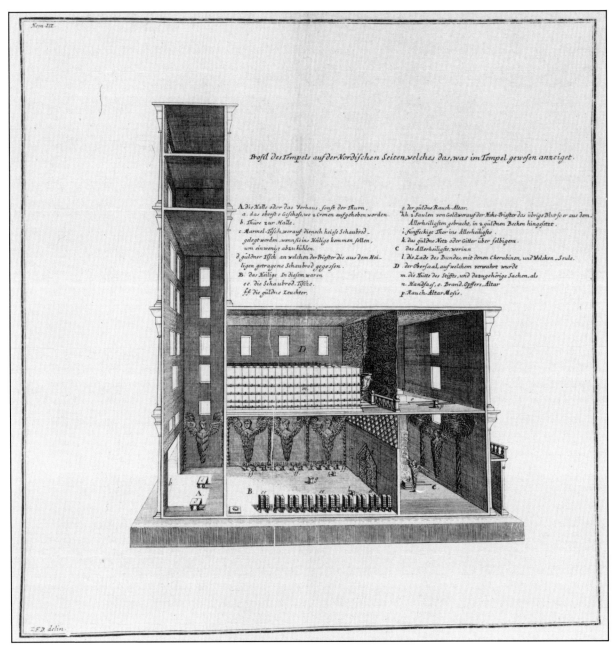

54. Profil des Tempels auf der Nordischen Seiten
(Profile of the North Side of the Temple)
From *Der Tempel Salomonis*
Drawn by I.F.D.
Printed by Wäysen-Haus
Halle, 1718
RB 416:7a

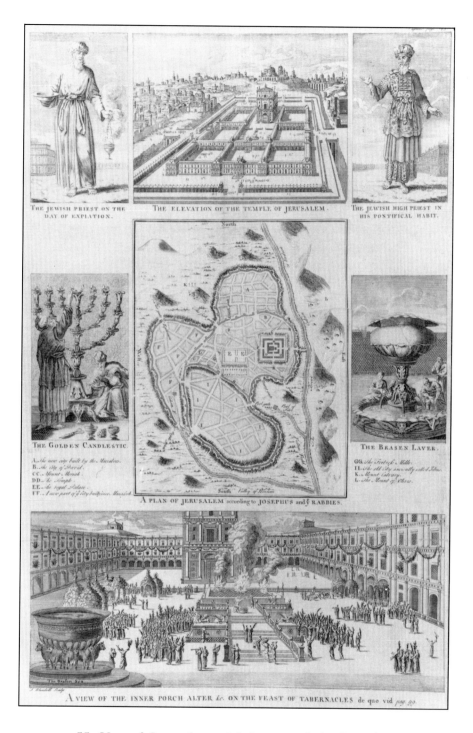

THE JEWISH PRIEST ON THE DAY OF EXPIATION.

THE ELEVATION OF THE TEMPLE OF JERUSALEM.

THE JEWISH HIGH PRIEST IN HIS PONTIFICAL HABIT.

THE GOLDEN CANDLESTIC.

THE BRASEN LAVER.

North

South Valley of Hinnom

A PLAN OF JERUSALEM according to JOSEPHUS and ye RABBIES.

A.. the new city built by the Macabees.
B.. the City of David.
CC.. Mount Moriah.
DD.. the Temple.
EE.. the royal Palace.
FF.. A new part of ye city built since Manasseh.

GG.. the Fortress Antonia.
H.. the old City anciently called Salem.
K.. Mount Calvary.
L.. the Mount of Olives.

A VIEW OF THE INNER PORCH ALTER &c. ON THE FEAST OF TABERNACLES de quo vid pag. 99

55. Map of Jerusalem with Images of the Temple
Engraved by J. Blundell
England, 18th century
(NS) Op 67

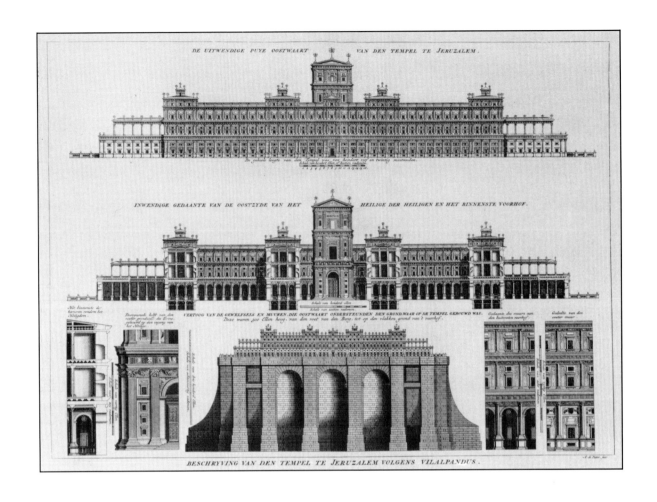

56. **Beschryving van den Tempel Te Jeruzalem Volgens Vilalpandus**
(Description of the Jerusalem Temple According to Villalpando)
Engraved by A. de Putter
Holland?, ca. 1730
M 66

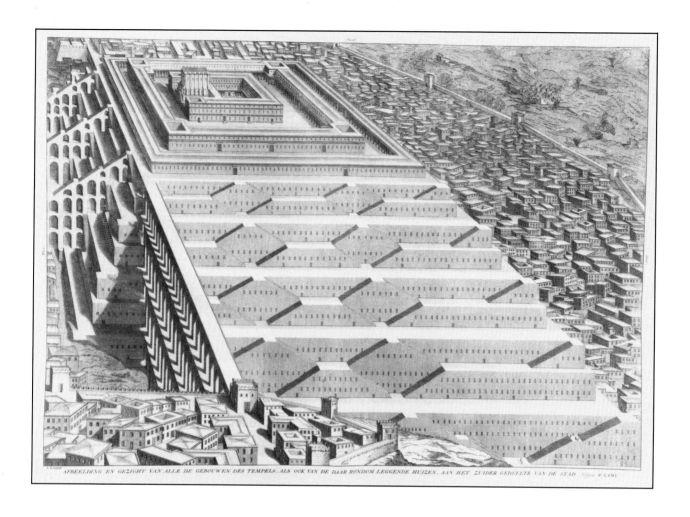

AFBEELDING EN GEZIGHT VAN ALLE DE GEBOUWEN DES TEMPELS, ALS OOK VAN DE DAAR RONDOM LEGGENDE HUIZEN, AAN HET ZUIDER GEDEELTE VAN DE STAD. *Volgens P. LAMY.*

57. **Afbeelding En Gezight Van Alle De Gebouwen Des Tempels . . . Volgens P. Lamy**
(Frontal View of All Buildings of the Temple . . . According to P. Lamy)
Holland?, ca. 1730
Engraved by A. de Putter
(NS) Op 15

58. **Micrographic Mizraḥ**
Elijah Mordeḥai Schor
Jerusalem, 19th century
Mc 24

59. **Amulet for Guarding the Home**
Moses ben Isaac Mizraḥi
Jerusalem, 19th century
P 21a

60. **Mizraḥ**
Moses ben Isaac Mizraḥi
Jerusalem, 19th century
P 20

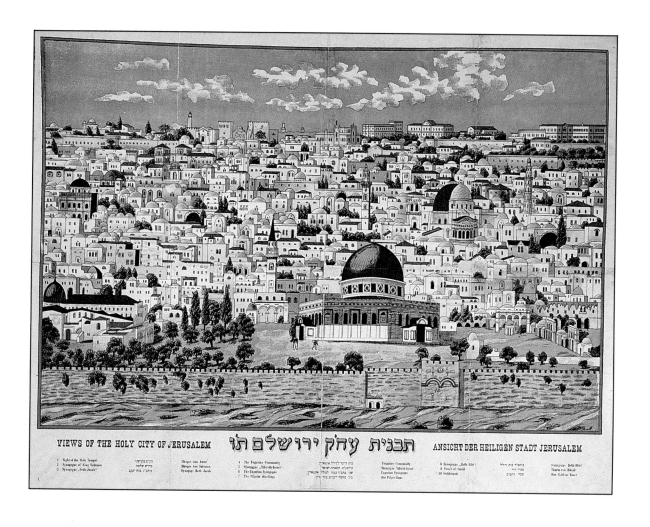

61. **Views of the Holy City of Jerusalem/**
Tavnit Ir ha-Kodesh Yerusalayim/Ansicht Der Heiligen Stadt Jerusalem
Jerusalem?, 20th century
M 191